Mastering Remote Work: Strategies for Success in a Digital World

By Anthony Colasante

Table of Contents

Introduction

1. **The Rise of Remote Work**
   - The Shift to Digital Workspaces
   - Benefits and Challenges of Remote Work

   Who This Guide is For

Chapter 1: Setting Up for Success

- **Creating the Ideal Workspace**
  - Choosing the Right Location
  - Essential Tools and Technology
  - Ergonomics and Comfort
- **Establishing a Daily Routine**
  - Morning Rituals for a Productive Day
  - Time Blocking and Task Management

  Dealing with Distractions

Chapter 2: Productivity Hacks for Remote Workers

- **Mastering Time Management**
  -

- The Pomodoro Technique
- Prioritization: The Eisenhower Matrix
- Digital Tools for Task Management

- **Staying Focused and Motivated**
  - Techniques to Avoid Procrastination
  - Goal Setting and Progress Tracking
  - The Importance of Breaks and Downtime

Chapter 3: Effective Communication in Remote Teams

- **Communication Tools and Platforms**
  - Selecting the Right Communication Channels
  - Video Conferencing Best Practices
  - Instant Messaging Etiquette

- **Building Strong Team Connections**
  - Fostering Collaboration in a Virtual Environment
  - Virtual Team-Building Activities
  - Managing Different Time Zones

- **Overcoming Communication Barriers**
  - Addressing Miscommunication

Cultivating Empathy and Understanding
    -

    Handling Conflicts Remotely

Chapter 4: Maintaining Work-Life Balance

- **Setting Boundaries**
    - Defining Work Hours and Personal Time
    - Communicating Boundaries with Family and Colleagues
    - Avoiding Burnout
- **Mindfulness and Mental Well-being**
    - Practices to Stay Centered and Calm
    - Managing Stress in a Remote Setting
    - Seeking Support When Needed
- **Work-Life Integration Strategies**
    - Blending Personal and Professional Goals
    - Creating Flexibility in Your Schedule
    - The Role of Hobbies and Personal Projects

Chapter 5: Long-term Success and Growth

- **Career Development in a Remote World**
    -

- Continuing Education and Skill Building
- Networking in a Remote Environment
- Advancing Your Career Remotely
- **Adapting to Change and Future Trends**
  - Staying Agile in an Evolving Workplace
  - The Future of Remote Work
  - Preparing for New Challenges

Conclusion

- **Your Roadmap to Remote Work Success**
  - Recap of Key Takeaways
  - Final Tips for Thriving Remotely
  - Resources for Continued Learning

Appendices

- **Appendix A: Recommended Tools and Resources**
  - Productivity Tools
  - Communication Platforms
  - Wellness and Mental Health Resources
- **Appendix B: Sample Templates and Checklists**

- Daily and Weekly Planning Templates
- Communication Protocols for Remote Teams
- Work-Life Balance Checklist

- **Appendix C: Further Reading and References**
  - Books, Articles, and Research Papers
  - Relevant Blogs and Websites
  - Podcasts and Videos on Remote Work

Introduction

The Rise of Remote Work

The world of work is undergoing a profound transformation. What was once considered an unconventional way to work—telecommuting or working from home—has now become mainstream. Remote work, accelerated by technological advancements and a global pandemic, is no longer just a trend; it's a significant shift in how we think about work and productivity.

In recent years, companies across the globe have embraced remote work as a viable and often preferable option. It's a shift that has empowered employees with greater flexibility, allowing them to work from anywhere, whether it's from the comfort of their home, a co-working space, or even while traveling. This new way of working has broken down geographical barriers, enabling companies to tap into a global talent pool and providing workers with opportunities that were previously out of reach.

However, this shift also brings challenges. As remote work becomes more prevalent, it demands new skills, strategies, and mindsets from both employees and employers. This guide is designed to help you navigate this new landscape and equip you with the tools you need to thrive in a remote work environment.

The Shift to Digital Workspaces

At the heart of remote work is the digital workspace—a virtual environment where collaboration, communication, and productivity take place without the need for a physical office. Digital workspaces leverage cloud-based tools and software to facilitate everything from project management and file sharing to video conferencing and team communication.

This shift to digital workspaces has transformed how businesses operate. Teams no longer need to be in the same location to collaborate effectively. Meetings can happen across time zones, documents can be edited in real-time by multiple people, and decisions can be made quickly and efficiently without the constraints of traditional office settings.

For employees, the digital workspace offers unprecedented flexibility. You can create a personalized work environment that suits your preferences, work during your most productive hours, and achieve a better work-life balance. However, the shift to digital also requires new ways of thinking about work. It's essential to stay connected, communicate effectively, and manage your time wisely in a digital environment where the lines between work and personal life can easily blur.

Benefits and Challenges of Remote Work

Remote work offers a multitude of benefits, both for employees and employers. For workers, the ability to work from anywhere provides a greater sense of autonomy and control over one's schedule. This flexibility often leads to increased job satisfaction, as employees can better balance their personal and professional lives. Additionally, remote work can lead to cost savings on commuting, office attire, and even meals.

For companies, remote work can reduce overhead costs associated with maintaining a physical office space. It also allows access to a broader talent pool, as businesses are no longer limited to hiring within a specific geographic area. This can lead to more diverse and innovative teams.

However, remote work is not without its challenges. One of the most significant hurdles is the potential for isolation. Without the social interactions that come naturally in an office environment, remote workers may feel disconnected from their colleagues and the company culture. This isolation can lead to decreased morale and productivity if not addressed.

Another challenge is maintaining a work-life balance. When your home becomes your office, it can be difficult to separate work time from personal time. This blurring of boundaries can lead to burnout if not managed properly.

Communication is another critical area where remote work presents challenges. Without face-to-face interactions, it's easy for misunderstandings to occur. Clear and effective communication becomes even more important in a remote setting to ensure that everyone is on the same page and that projects move forward smoothly.

This guide will provide strategies to overcome these challenges, helping you harness the benefits of remote work while avoiding the pitfalls.

Who This Guide is For

This guide is designed for anyone who is navigating the world of remote work, whether you're a seasoned professional or new to working from home. It's for employees who want to maximize their productivity and well-being in a remote setting, as well as for managers and team leaders who are responsible for guiding remote teams to success.

If you're struggling with the challenges of remote work—be it finding the right balance between work and life, staying productive, or maintaining strong communication with your team—this guide will offer practical advice and actionable strategies to help you succeed.

Whether you're working remotely by choice or necessity, this guide aims to empower you with the knowledge and tools you need to thrive in a digital workspace. From setting up your home office to mastering time management and communication, this guide covers all aspects of remote work, providing a comprehensive roadmap to success in this new era of work.

Chapter 1: Setting Up for Success

Creating the Ideal Workspace

In the world of remote work, your environment can significantly impact your productivity and well-being. Unlike traditional office spaces, where your workspace is typically predefined, working remotely gives you the flexibility to create a personalized environment that suits your needs. Here's how to set up a workspace that fosters success.

Choosing the Right Location

The first step in creating an ideal workspace is selecting the right location within your home or wherever you plan to work. Ideally, this space should be quiet, free from distractions, and away from high-traffic areas. If possible, choose a room with a door you can close to signal to others (and yourself) that you are in work mode.

Natural light is another important factor to consider. A well-lit space can boost your mood and energy levels, making you more productive throughout the day. Position your desk near a window to take advantage of natural light, but ensure that glare from the sun doesn't affect your computer screen.

If space is limited, get creative. Consider using room dividers to carve out a dedicated work area, or repurpose a nook or corner into your new office. The key is to create a space that helps you focus and feel comfortable during your work hours.

Essential Tools and Technology

Having the right tools and technology is crucial to remote work success. Start with the basics: a reliable computer and high-speed internet connection. These are non-negotiable, as they form the backbone of your ability to work efficiently.

Next, think about the peripherals. A comfortable, ergonomic chair and a desk at the right height are investments worth making to prevent strain and injury. If you're working from a laptop, consider getting an external monitor, keyboard, and mouse to create a more ergonomic setup.

Other essential tools might include noise-canceling headphones to block out background noise, a webcam for video calls, and a good microphone for clear communication. Don't forget about software—ensure you have access to the necessary productivity apps, communication platforms, and security software to protect your work.

Ergonomics and Comfort

Ergonomics play a vital role in maintaining your physical health while working remotely. Poor ergonomics can lead to issues like back pain, neck strain, and repetitive stress injuries, all of which can impact your productivity and quality of life.

Start with your chair. It should support your lower back and allow your feet to rest flat on the floor. Adjust the height of your chair so that your elbows are at a 90-degree angle when typing, and your wrists are straight.

Your monitor should be at eye level, about an arm's length away. If you're using a laptop, elevate it with a stand or stack of books and use an external keyboard and mouse. This setup will help prevent neck and shoulder strain.

Consider using a standing desk or a convertible desk that allows you to switch between sitting and standing. This can reduce the negative effects of prolonged sitting and keep your energy levels up.

Lastly, make your workspace comfortable and inspiring. Add personal touches like plants, artwork, or photos that make you feel good. Keep the space tidy and organized to reduce stress and improve focus.

Establishing a Daily Routine

A daily routine is the backbone of productivity, especially in a remote work environment where the lines between work and personal life can easily blur. Establishing a routine helps you create structure, stay on track with your tasks, and maintain a healthy work-life balance.

Morning Rituals for a Productive Day

How you start your day sets the tone for the rest of it. Establishing a consistent morning routine can help you transition from home mode to work mode, even if you're only moving from your kitchen to your home office.

Begin with activities that energize you. This could be a morning workout, meditation, or simply enjoying a cup of coffee while reading the news. The goal is to wake up your body and mind, setting a positive tone for the day ahead.

Set a specific time to start work each day and stick to it. This helps create a sense of normalcy and signals to your brain that it's time to focus. Before diving into tasks, take a few minutes to review your goals for the day, prioritize your tasks, and create a to-do list. This practice will give you a clear roadmap for the day, helping you stay focused and productive.

Time Blocking and Task Management

Time blocking is a powerful technique for managing your day and ensuring that you stay productive. It involves dividing your day into blocks of time, each dedicated to a specific task or group of tasks. By scheduling your workday in this way, you can minimize distractions and ensure that you're making steady progress on your projects.

Start by identifying your most important tasks—the ones that will have the biggest impact on your goals. Block out time for these tasks during your peak productivity hours, which are typically in the morning for most people. Dedicate specific blocks of time for meetings, emails, and other administrative tasks, ensuring they don't interrupt your focus on key projects.

It's also important to schedule breaks throughout the day. Short breaks can help you recharge and maintain your focus. Use techniques like the Pomodoro method, which involves working for 25 minutes and then taking a 5-minute break, to maintain a rhythm that keeps you productive without burning out.

Dealing with Distractions

Distractions are one of the biggest challenges of remote work, especially when working from home. Whether it's household chores, family members, or social media, it's easy to get sidetracked.

To minimize distractions, set clear boundaries with those you live with. Let them know your work hours and ask them to respect your workspace during these times. If noise is an issue, use noise-canceling headphones or a white noise machine to create a more focused environment.

Social media and digital distractions can also be major productivity killers. Consider using apps that block distracting websites during work hours or setting your phone to "Do Not Disturb" mode. Schedule specific times to check your email and social media, rather than allowing them to interrupt your workflow throughout the day.

It's also helpful to create a ritual for starting and ending your workday. This could be something as simple as shutting down your computer at the end of the day and physically leaving your workspace. These rituals signal to your brain that it's time to switch between work and personal life, helping you maintain better focus during work hours and enjoy your time off.

By creating an ideal workspace, establishing a productive routine, and effectively managing distractions, you lay a strong foundation for remote work success. In the next chapter, we'll dive deeper into specific productivity hacks that can help you maximize your efficiency and achieve your goals in a remote work environment.

Chapter 2: Productivity Hacks for Remote Workers

Remote work offers the freedom to manage your time and tasks in ways that suit you best. However, this flexibility can be a double-edged sword if not managed effectively. In this chapter, we'll explore productivity hacks that can help you make the most of your remote work environment, ensuring that you stay on track, meet your goals, and maintain a healthy work-life balance.

Mastering Time Management

Time management is the cornerstone of productivity, especially in a remote work setting where distractions are abundant and structure is self-imposed. Effective time management allows you to prioritize tasks, minimize stress, and maximize your output.

The Pomodoro Technique

One of the most popular and effective time management strategies is the Pomodoro Technique. Developed by Francesco Cirillo in the late 1980s, this method involves breaking your workday into 25-minute intervals called "Pomodoros," separated by 5-minute breaks. After four Pomodoros, you take a longer break of 15-30 minutes.

The beauty of the Pomodoro Technique lies in its simplicity. By focusing on a single task for a short, defined period, you can minimize distractions and procrastination. The frequent breaks help to prevent burnout and keep your mind fresh.

Here's how to implement the Pomodoro Technique:

1. **Choose a task**: Select a task you want to work on.
2. **Set a timer**: Set your timer for 25 minutes and focus solely on the task at hand.
3. **Work on the task**: Avoid distractions and work until the timer goes off.

4. **Take a short break**: Take a 5-minute break to rest and recharge.
5. **Repeat**: After four Pomodoros, take a longer break.

This method is particularly effective for tasks that require deep concentration, as it breaks them down into manageable chunks and makes the work feel less daunting.

Prioritization: The Eisenhower Matrix

Another essential aspect of time management is prioritization—knowing which tasks to tackle first and which can be delegated or postponed. The Eisenhower Matrix, also known as the Urgent-Important Matrix, is a powerful tool for this purpose.

The Eisenhower Matrix divides tasks into four quadrants:

1. **Urgent and Important**: Tasks that require immediate attention and have significant consequences. These should be your top priority.
2. **Important but Not Urgent**: Tasks that are important for your long-term goals but don't require immediate action. These should be scheduled for later.
3. **Urgent but Not Important**: Tasks that require immediate attention but don't contribute significantly to your goals. These can often be delegated to someone else.
4. **Not Urgent and Not Important**: Tasks that are neither urgent nor important. These are usually distractions that should be minimized or eliminated.

By categorizing your tasks using the Eisenhower Matrix, you can ensure that you're focusing your time and energy on what truly matters, rather than getting bogged down by less important tasks.

Digital Tools for Task Management

In a remote work environment, digital tools are invaluable for keeping track of tasks, deadlines, and projects. Here are some popular tools that can help you manage your workload effectively:

- **Trello**: A visual task management tool that uses boards, lists, and cards to organize tasks. Trello is great for both individual task management and team collaboration.
- **Asana**: A comprehensive project management tool that allows you to create tasks, set deadlines, assign tasks to team members, and track progress. It's particularly useful for managing complex projects with multiple stakeholders.
- **Todoist**: A simple yet powerful task management app that lets you create to-do lists, set priorities, and schedule tasks. Its clean interface makes it easy to stay organized.
- **Notion**: An all-in-one workspace where you can manage tasks, take notes, create databases, and collaborate with your team. Notion's flexibility makes it ideal for remote workers who need to manage multiple types of information in one place.

These tools can help you stay organized, ensure nothing falls through the cracks, and keep you on track to meet your goals.

Staying Focused and Motivated

Maintaining focus and motivation is one of the biggest challenges in remote work. Without the structure of a traditional office environment, it's easy to become distracted or lose momentum. However, with the right techniques, you can stay focused and motivated throughout your workday.

Techniques to Avoid Procrastination

Procrastination is a common pitfall in remote work, often fueled by the lack of immediate supervision and the presence of distractions. Here are some techniques to help you overcome procrastination:

- **The Two-Minute Rule**: If a task takes less than two minutes to complete, do it immediately. This prevents small tasks from piling up and becoming overwhelming.
- **The Five-Second Rule**: When you feel the urge to procrastinate, count down from five and then take action. This simple trick can help you break the inertia and get started on a task.
- **Time Blocking**: Dedicate specific blocks of time to different tasks. Knowing that you only have a limited time to complete a task can motivate you to start and stay focused.

Goal Setting and Progress Tracking

Setting clear, achievable goals is essential for staying motivated and maintaining momentum. Without goals, it's easy to lose sight of what you're working towards, leading to decreased productivity and motivation.

Start by setting long-term goals, then break them down into smaller, manageable tasks. This makes large projects feel less overwhelming and gives you a clear path to follow. Use the SMART criteria (Specific, Measurable, Achievable, Relevant, Time-bound) to ensure your goals are well-defined and attainable.

Progress tracking is equally important. Regularly reviewing your progress can boost your motivation, as it allows you to see how far you've come and what you've accomplished. It also helps you identify any areas where you might be falling behind, so you can adjust your strategy accordingly.

Tools like Asana, Trello, or even a simple spreadsheet can be useful for tracking your goals and progress. Some people also find it helpful to keep a journal where they record their achievements and reflect on their progress.

The Importance of Breaks and Downtime

While it's important to stay focused and productive, it's equally important to take breaks and allow yourself downtime. Without the natural breaks that come with working in an office—like chatting with colleagues or grabbing coffee—remote workers can easily fall into the trap of working non-stop, leading to burnout.

Taking regular breaks helps to maintain your energy levels and mental clarity. The Pomodoro Technique, as mentioned earlier, is one way to structure your breaks throughout the day. In addition to short breaks, it's also important to schedule longer breaks for meals and to step away from your workspace.

Downtime is crucial for recharging your mental and physical batteries. Make sure to disconnect from work at the end of the day and engage in activities that relax and rejuvenate you, whether it's spending time with family, exercising, or pursuing a hobby.

By mastering time management, staying focused, setting clear goals, and taking regular breaks, you can enhance your productivity and thrive as a remote worker. In the next chapter, we'll explore how to communicate effectively in remote teams, build strong connections, and overcome common communication barriers in a digital workspace.

Chapter 3: Effective Communication in Remote Teams

Communication is the backbone of any successful team, and it becomes even more crucial in a remote work environment. Without the ability to drop by a colleague's desk or have impromptu meetings in the hallway, remote teams must rely on digital tools and strategies to stay connected and collaborate effectively. In this chapter, we'll explore the key aspects of communication in remote teams, including selecting the right tools, building strong connections, and overcoming common communication barriers.

Communication Tools and Platforms

In a remote work environment, digital communication tools are essential for keeping teams connected, informed, and productive. However, with so many tools available, it's important to select the right ones for your team's needs.

Selecting the Right Communication Channels

The first step in effective communication is choosing the right channels for different types of communication. Each tool or platform serves a specific purpose, and using them appropriately can enhance clarity and efficiency.

- **Email**: Best for formal communication, detailed information, and documentation. Use email for messages that don't require an immediate response or when you need to share detailed information that can be referenced later.
- **Instant Messaging (e.g., Slack, Microsoft Teams)**: Ideal for quick, real-time communication. Instant messaging is perfect for quick questions, updates, and informal conversations. However, it's important to set boundaries to prevent it from becoming a distraction.

- **Video Conferencing (e.g., Zoom, Google Meet)**: Essential for meetings, presentations, and any communication that benefits from face-to-face interaction. Video conferencing helps build stronger connections and ensures that non-verbal cues, which are often lost in text communication, are conveyed.

- **Project Management Tools (e.g., Trello, Asana, Monday.com)**: These tools are crucial for keeping track of tasks, deadlines, and project progress. They help ensure that everyone is on the same page and that projects move forward smoothly.

Choosing the right communication channels and using them appropriately can significantly improve the efficiency and effectiveness of remote team communication.

Video Conferencing Best Practices

Video conferencing has become a cornerstone of remote work, allowing teams to meet face-to-face, no matter where they are. However, to make the most of video meetings, it's important to follow best practices:

- **Prepare in Advance**: Have an agenda and share it with participants before the meeting. This ensures that everyone knows what will be discussed and can prepare accordingly.
- **Test Your Technology**: Ensure that your camera, microphone, and internet connection are working properly before the meeting starts. This prevents technical issues from disrupting the meeting.

- **Dress Appropriately**: Even though you're working from home, dressing appropriately for video meetings helps set a professional tone and shows respect for your colleagues.
- **Be Mindful of Your Environment**: Choose a quiet, well-lit space for video calls. Make sure your background is free of distractions, and if possible, use a virtual background to maintain privacy.
- **Engage Actively**: Make an effort to engage with others during the meeting. Look at the camera when speaking to simulate eye contact, and use non-verbal cues like nodding to show that you're listening.
-

  Follow Up: After the meeting, send a summary of the key points discussed and any action items. This helps ensure that everyone is on the same page and knows what to do next.

Instant Messaging Etiquette

Instant messaging is a valuable tool for quick communication, but it can also be a source of distraction if not used properly. Here are some tips for maintaining good etiquette in instant messaging:

- **Be Respectful of Others' Time**: Before sending a message, consider whether it's the best time to reach out. If the message isn't urgent, it might be better to send an email or schedule a time to chat.
- **Keep Messages Concise**: Get to the point quickly. Long, rambling messages can be overwhelming and may be overlooked. If a discussion requires more depth, consider moving it to a call or video meeting.
-

- **Use Status Indicators**: If your messaging platform has status indicators (e.g., available, busy, away), use them to signal your availability. Respect others' status indicators as well.
- **Avoid Multitasking**: When engaging in a chat, focus on the conversation. Multitasking during a chat can lead to miscommunication and missed details.
- **Set Boundaries**: To prevent instant messaging from becoming a constant interruption, set specific times for checking and responding to messages. Let your team know your availability so they can plan accordingly.

Building Strong Team Connections

One of the challenges of remote work is building and maintaining strong team connections. Without the benefit of in-person interactions, it's important to be intentional about fostering a sense of camaraderie and collaboration within the team.

Fostering Collaboration in a Virtual Environment

Effective collaboration is key to the success of any team, and it's particularly important in a remote setting where team members may be working independently much of the time. Here are some strategies to foster collaboration in a virtual environment:

- **Regular Check-Ins**: Schedule regular team meetings to discuss progress, address any challenges, and keep everyone aligned on goals. These meetings are also an opportunity for team members to share ideas and offer support.
- **Use Collaborative Tools**: Make use of digital tools that allow for real-time collaboration, such as shared

documents, virtual whiteboards, and project management platforms. These tools make it easier for team members to work together, even when they're not in the same location.

- **Encourage Open Communication**: Create an environment where team members feel comfortable sharing their thoughts and ideas. Encourage open communication and make it clear that all contributions are valued.

- **Promote a Culture of Trust**: Trust is essential for effective collaboration. Foster trust by being transparent, following through on commitments, and supporting your team members.

Virtual Team-Building Activities

Team-building activities are important for strengthening relationships within a team, and they're just as valuable in a remote setting as they are in an office. Here are some ideas for virtual team-building activities:

- **Virtual Coffee Breaks**: Schedule regular informal coffee breaks where team members can chat and catch up. These breaks provide an opportunity for social interaction and help to build stronger connections.

- **Online Games and Challenges**: Organize online games or challenges that the team can participate in together. This could be anything from a virtual trivia quiz to an online escape room.

- **Share Personal Updates**: Dedicate a portion of team meetings to sharing personal updates or achievements. This helps team members get to know each other on a more personal level.

-

Virtual Workshops or Learning Sessions: Arrange virtual workshops or learning sessions where team members can share their expertise or learn something new together. This not only builds skills but also fosters a sense of community.

Managing Different Time Zones

When working with a distributed team, managing different time zones can be a challenge. It requires careful planning and consideration to ensure that everyone feels included and that communication remains smooth.

- **Use Time Zone Tools**: Tools like World Time Buddy or Google Calendar can help you easily see what time it is in different locations. This is useful for scheduling meetings that accommodate everyone's time zone.
- **Rotate Meeting Times**: If your team spans multiple time zones, consider rotating meeting times so that no one group is consistently inconvenienced. This helps distribute the burden of early or late meetings more evenly.
- **Record Meetings**: If someone can't attend a meeting due to time zone differences, record the meeting so they can watch it later. Provide a summary and action items as well.
- **Asynchronous Communication**: Encourage the use of asynchronous communication (e.g., email, project management tools) for tasks that don't require immediate feedback. This allows team members to contribute at times that work best for them.

Overcoming Communication Barriers

Effective communication is essential, but it's not always easy, especially in a remote work environment. Miscommunication, misunderstandings, and conflicts can arise if communication isn't handled carefully.

Addressing Miscommunication

Miscommunication is one of the most common issues in remote teams, often caused by the lack of non-verbal cues and the reliance on written communication. Here's how to address and prevent miscommunication:

- **Be Clear and Concise**: When communicating in writing, be as clear and concise as possible. Avoid jargon and be specific about what you need or what you're asking.
- **Ask for Clarification**: If you're unsure about something, don't hesitate to ask for clarification. It's better to ask questions than to make assumptions that could lead to misunderstandings.
- **Use Visuals**: When explaining complex ideas, consider using visuals like diagrams, charts, or screenshots to help convey your message more clearly.
- **Summarize and Confirm**: At the end of a conversation or meeting, summarize the key points and confirm that everyone is on the same page. This helps ensure that everyone has the same understanding of what was discussed.

Cultivating Empathy and Understanding

Empathy and understanding are crucial for maintaining positive relationships within a remote team. Without the ability to pick up on non-verbal cues, it's important to be mindful of how others might be feeling and to approach communication with empathy.

- **Listen Actively**: Make an effort to listen actively during conversations. This means paying full attention to the speaker, acknowledging their points, and responding thoughtfully.
- **Consider Others' Perspectives**: Before responding, consider the other person's perspective. This can help you communicate more empathetically and avoid potential conflicts.
- **Be Supportive**: Offer support to your team members when they're facing challenges. Whether it's a work-related issue or a personal matter, showing that you care can go a long way in building strong, trusting relationships.

Handling Conflicts Remotely

Conflicts are inevitable in any team, but they can be particularly challenging to manage in a remote setting. Without the ability to resolve issues face-to-face, it's important to approach conflict resolution thoughtfully and carefully.

- **Address Issues Early**: Don't let conflicts fester. Address issues as soon as they arise, before they have a chance to escalate.
- **Use Video Calls for Difficult Conversations**: When dealing with a conflict, use video calls rather than written communication. This allows for more nuanced communication and helps to build understanding.
-

Focus on the Issue, Not the Person: When resolving conflicts, focus on the specific issue at hand rather than personalizing the conflict. This helps to keep the conversation constructive and focused on finding a solution.
-

Seek to Understand: Before jumping to conclusions, seek to understand the other person's perspective. This can help you identify the root cause of the conflict and find a resolution that works for everyone.

Effective communication is key to the success of any remote team. By choosing the right tools, fostering collaboration, and handling communication challenges with care, you can build strong, connected teams that work together seamlessly, no matter where they are. In the next chapter, we'll explore how to maintain a healthy work-life balance while working remotely, setting boundaries, and prioritizing well-being.

Chapter 4: Maintaining Work-Life Balance

Remote work offers the flexibility to create a work environment that suits your personal and professional needs. However, without the physical separation between home and office, the lines between work and personal life can easily blur. Maintaining a healthy work-life balance is crucial for your well-being and long-term productivity. In this chapter, we'll explore strategies for setting boundaries, managing stress, and integrating your work and personal life in a way that enhances both.

Setting Boundaries

One of the most significant challenges of remote work is setting clear boundaries between work and personal life. Without the natural cues of a commute or a designated office space, it's easy to find yourself working late into the evening or checking emails during personal time. Establishing boundaries is essential to ensure that work doesn't take over your life.

Defining Work Hours and Personal Time

The first step in setting boundaries is defining your work hours. Just as you would in a traditional office setting, establish specific start and end times for your workday. This not only helps you stay productive during work hours but also ensures that you have time to unwind and focus on personal activities.

Once you've established your work hours, stick to them as much as possible. It can be tempting to keep working when you're in the middle of a project or to start early to get a head start on the day, but this can quickly lead to burnout. Treat your work hours as non-negotiable, and use your personal time to recharge.

Communicating Boundaries with Family and Colleagues

Clear communication is key to maintaining boundaries, especially when others are involved. Let your family members or housemates know your work schedule and ask them to respect your work hours. If possible, designate a specific area of your home as your workspace, and make it clear that when you're in that space, you're not to be disturbed.

Similarly, communicate your boundaries to your colleagues. Let them know when you're available and when you're not, and encourage them to respect these boundaries. If you're working across different time zones, make sure your colleagues are aware of your time zone and availability.

It's also important to be firm about your boundaries. If someone tries to contact you outside of your work hours, don't feel obligated to respond immediately. You can politely let them know that you'll get back to them during your next workday.

Avoiding Burnout

Burnout is a common risk in remote work, especially when boundaries are not well established. It's important to recognize the signs of burnout—such as chronic fatigue, irritability, and a sense of being overwhelmed—and take proactive steps to prevent it.

One of the most effective ways to avoid burnout is to take regular breaks throughout the day. As mentioned in previous chapters, techniques like the Pomodoro Technique can help you structure your workday in a way that includes frequent, short breaks. These breaks give you a chance to step away from your work, relax, and recharge.

In addition to daily breaks, make sure to take time off when needed. Whether it's a long weekend or a full vacation, time away from work is crucial for maintaining your mental and physical health. Don't hesitate to use your vacation days, and encourage your team members to do the same.

Mindfulness and Mental Well-being

Maintaining your mental well-being is essential for sustaining a healthy work-life balance. Mindfulness practices can help you stay centered and calm, even in the face of stress and challenges.

Practices to Stay Centered and Calm

Mindfulness involves paying attention to the present moment without judgment. It can be practiced in various ways, from meditation and deep breathing exercises to simply taking a moment to notice your surroundings and sensations.

One simple mindfulness practice is to start your day with a few minutes of deep breathing or meditation. This can help you set a positive tone for the day and reduce stress. Throughout the day, take short mindfulness breaks to check in with yourself, notice how you're feeling, and re-center your focus.

Another effective practice is mindful walking. If possible, take a walk outside during your breaks or after your workday. Focus on the sensations of walking—the feeling of your feet on the ground, the rhythm of your breath, and the sights and sounds around you. This can help clear your mind and reduce stress.

Managing Stress in a Remote Setting

Stress is inevitable, but it's important to manage it effectively to prevent it from impacting your work and personal life. In a remote setting, where you might be dealing with isolation or the pressure to always be "on," stress management becomes even more crucial.

One effective strategy for managing stress is to create a structured routine that includes time for relaxation and self-care. This might include activities like exercise, reading, hobbies, or spending time with loved ones. Make sure these activities are part of your daily or weekly schedule, and treat them as non-negotiable.

Another key to managing stress is to recognize when you need help. If you're feeling overwhelmed, don't hesitate to reach out to a friend, family member, or mental health professional. Sometimes, just talking about what you're going through can help relieve some of the pressure.

Seeking Support When Needed

Working remotely doesn't mean you have to go it alone. It's important to have a support system in place, whether it's friends, family, colleagues, or professional resources.

If you're struggling with work-related stress, consider reaching out to a colleague or manager. They may be able to offer support, advice, or adjustments to your workload. Many companies also offer Employee Assistance Programs (EAPs) that provide counseling and mental health resources.

In your personal life, make sure to stay connected with friends and family. Even if you're physically distant, regular video calls, phone calls, or messaging can help you feel more connected and supported.

Work-Life Integration Strategies

While setting boundaries is important, it's also essential to find ways to integrate your work and personal life in a way that feels harmonious. Work-life integration focuses on blending your professional and personal goals in a way that enhances both.

Blending Personal and Professional Goals

Work-life integration involves finding ways to align your personal and professional goals, so they complement each other. For example, if personal development is important to you, you might set professional goals that allow you to learn new skills or take on new challenges.

Similarly, if spending more time with family is a priority, look for ways to structure your workday that allow for family time. This might involve starting work earlier so you can finish earlier, or taking a longer break in the afternoon to spend time with your kids.

By aligning your work and personal goals, you can create a sense of balance and fulfillment that benefits both areas of your life.

Creating Flexibility in Your Schedule

One of the biggest advantages of remote work is the ability to create a flexible schedule that suits your needs. Take advantage of this flexibility by designing a schedule that allows you to work during your most productive hours while also making time for personal activities.

For example, if you're a morning person, you might choose to start work early and finish by mid-afternoon, leaving the rest of the day for personal pursuits. Alternatively, if you're more productive in the evening, you might structure your day to allow for a longer break in the middle, with work continuing into the evening.

Flexibility also means being adaptable. Some days might require more focus on work, while others might allow for more personal time. The key is to create a schedule that works for you and to adjust it as needed.

The Role of Hobbies and Personal Projects

Hobbies and personal projects play a crucial role in maintaining a healthy work-life balance. They provide an outlet for creativity, relaxation, and personal growth, which are all essential for overall well-being.

Make time for hobbies and personal projects, and treat them as an important part of your routine. Whether it's painting, gardening, writing, or learning a new skill, these activities can help you recharge and bring a sense of satisfaction and fulfillment.

Engaging in hobbies also helps prevent burnout by giving you something to look forward to outside of work. They allow you to express yourself in ways that are different from your professional role, which can lead to a more balanced and enriched life.

Maintaining work-life balance in a remote work environment requires intentionality and effort. By setting boundaries, managing stress, integrating your work and personal goals, and making time for relaxation and hobbies, you can create a fulfilling and sustainable lifestyle that supports both your professional and personal well-being. In the next chapter, we'll explore long-term strategies for success and growth in remote work, including career development and adapting to future trends.

Chapter 5: Long-term Success and Growth

As remote work becomes a permanent fixture in the professional landscape, it's essential to think about your long-term success and growth in this environment. Whether you're looking to advance in your current role, develop new skills, or adapt to the changing nature of work, this chapter will provide strategies to help you thrive over the long term.

Career Development in a Remote World

Remote work offers unique opportunities for career development, but it also requires a proactive approach. Without the traditional office environment, you'll need to take charge of your growth by seeking out opportunities, building your network, and continuously developing your skills.

Continuing Education and Skill Building

In a rapidly changing work environment, continuous learning is crucial. Remote work often provides more flexibility, making it easier to pursue additional education or skill development alongside your job. Here's how to make the most of these opportunities:

- **Identify Key Skills**: Start by identifying the skills that are most valuable in your field or the ones you need to advance your career. This could include technical skills, such as coding or data analysis, or soft skills, like leadership and communication.
- **Online Courses and Certifications**: Take advantage of the wide range of online courses and certifications available. Platforms like Coursera, Udemy, LinkedIn Learning, and edX offer courses in almost every field. Earning certifications in relevant areas can enhance your

resume and demonstrate your commitment to professional growth.

- **Attend Virtual Workshops and Webinars**: Many organizations and educational institutions offer virtual workshops and webinars. These can be great opportunities to learn from industry experts and stay up-to-date with the latest trends and best practices.

- **Set Learning Goals**: Incorporate skill-building into your routine by setting specific learning goals. Whether it's completing a course, reading industry-related books, or mastering a new tool, having clear objectives will help you stay focused and motivated.

Networking in a Remote Environment

Networking is a vital component of career development, but it can be more challenging in a remote setting where you don't have the same opportunities for casual interactions. However, with a little effort, you can build and maintain a strong professional network remotely.

- **Leverage Social Media**: Platforms like LinkedIn, Twitter, and professional forums are excellent for connecting with others in your field. Engage with content, join discussions, and reach out to industry leaders and peers to build your network.

- **Participate in Online Communities**: Join online communities and groups related to your industry. These can be found on platforms like LinkedIn, Slack, or even Reddit. Active participation in these communities can lead to valuable connections and insights.

-

- **Attend Virtual Conferences and Meetups**: Many conferences and industry events have moved online, making it easier to attend without the need for travel. These events offer opportunities to learn, network, and even present your work to a wider audience.

- **Build Relationships Within Your Organization**: Don't neglect networking within your current organization. Regularly check in with colleagues, attend virtual team-building activities, and seek out mentorship opportunities. Building strong internal relationships can open doors to new opportunities and career advancement.

Advancing Your Career Remotely

Advancing your career in a remote environment requires a strategic approach. Without the visibility that comes from being in an office, you'll need to be intentional about demonstrating your value and seeking out new opportunities.

- **Showcase Your Achievements**: Make sure your contributions are visible to your team and leadership. Regularly update your manager on your progress, share your successes during team meetings, and document your achievements in performance reviews.

- **Seek Out New Responsibilities**: Look for opportunities to take on new responsibilities or lead projects. This not only demonstrates your initiative but also helps you develop new skills and gain experience in different areas.

- **Build a Personal Brand**: Establish yourself as an expert in your field by creating content, such as blog posts, articles, or videos, and sharing them on professional platforms. Building a personal brand can enhance your reputation and open up new opportunities.

- **Ask for Feedback and Act on It**: Regularly seek feedback from your manager and colleagues, and use it to improve your performance. Demonstrating a willingness to learn and grow is key to advancing in your career.
- **Plan Your Career Path**: Take time to plan your career path, setting both short-term and long-term goals. Consider where you want to be in the next few years and what steps you need to take to get there. This might involve gaining specific skills, taking on new roles, or transitioning to a different field.

Adapting to Change and Future Trends

The workplace is evolving rapidly, and staying agile is essential for long-term success. As remote work continues to grow, it's important to keep an eye on future trends and be prepared to adapt to new challenges.

Staying Agile in an Evolving Workplace

Agility is the ability to adapt quickly to changes in your work environment. In a remote work setting, this might involve learning new tools, adjusting to different ways of working, or taking on new responsibilities.

- **Stay Informed**: Keep up-to-date with the latest trends and developments in your industry. Subscribe to industry newsletters, follow thought leaders, and participate in relevant online discussions.
- **Embrace Change**: Be open to change and willing to experiment with new tools and methods. The ability to quickly adapt to new technologies and processes will make you more valuable in any work environment.

- **Develop Problem-Solving Skills**: The ability to solve problems creatively and efficiently is a key aspect of agility. Practice critical thinking and look for opportunities to improve processes or address challenges in your work.
- **Cultivate a Growth Mindset**: A growth mindset is the belief that your abilities can be developed through hard work, learning, and persistence. Embrace challenges, learn from setbacks, and continuously seek opportunities to grow.

The Future of Remote Work

The future of work is likely to be a hybrid of remote and in-office work, with flexibility becoming a key feature of many jobs. Here are some trends to watch:

- **Hybrid Work Models**: Many companies are adopting hybrid work models, where employees split their time between working remotely and working in the office. Understanding how to navigate this model will be crucial.
- **Increased Use of AI and Automation**: As AI and automation technologies continue to evolve, they will play a larger role in the workplace. Staying informed about these technologies and learning how to work alongside them will be important for staying competitive.
- **Focus on Employee Well-being**: Companies are increasingly recognizing the importance of employee well-being, particularly in remote work settings. Expect to see more emphasis on mental health support, work-life balance, and flexible working arrangements.
-

Global Talent Pools: Remote work allows companies to hire talent from anywhere in the world. This means increased competition, but also more opportunities for those willing to work remotely for companies in different locations.

Preparing for New Challenges

As remote work continues to evolve, new challenges will inevitably arise. Being prepared to face these challenges head-on will set you apart as a leader and a valuable team member.

- **Stay Adaptable**: Be ready to adapt to new technologies, work processes, and industry trends. Flexibility will be key to navigating the future of work.
- **Invest in Lifelong Learning**: The need for continuous learning will only grow as the workplace evolves. Make a commitment to lifelong learning and stay curious about new developments in your field.
- **Cultivate Resilience**: Resilience is the ability to bounce back from setbacks and continue moving forward. Developing resilience will help you navigate the ups and downs of your career, particularly in a rapidly changing work environment.
- **Build a Strong Professional Network**: Your professional network will be an invaluable resource as you navigate new challenges and opportunities. Continue to build and nurture relationships with others in your field.

Long-term success and growth in a remote work environment require a proactive approach to career development, a willingness to adapt to change, and a commitment to continuous learning. By investing in your skills, building your network, and staying agile, you can thrive in the evolving world of remote work and achieve your career goals. As you move forward, keep an eye on future trends, stay adaptable, and embrace the opportunities that remote work offers.

Conclusion

Your Roadmap to Remote Work Success

As remote work becomes an integral part of the modern professional landscape, it's more important than ever to master the skills and strategies necessary to thrive in this environment. Throughout this guide, we've explored the various aspects of remote work, from setting up an ideal workspace to managing your time effectively, communicating with remote teams, maintaining a healthy work-life balance, and positioning yourself for long-term success.

By integrating these strategies into your daily routine, you can create a productive, fulfilling, and sustainable remote work experience that supports both your professional and personal goals.

Recap of Key Takeaways

Let's revisit the key takeaways from each chapter of this guide:

1. **Setting Up for Success**: Your workspace and routine are the foundation of your remote work success. Choose a dedicated workspace, invest in the right tools, and establish a daily routine that maximizes productivity while maintaining comfort.
2. **Productivity Hacks**: Effective time management is crucial. Utilize techniques like the Pomodoro Technique, prioritize tasks using the Eisenhower Matrix, and leverage digital tools to stay organized and focused. Remember to take regular breaks to prevent burnout and maintain your well-being.
3. **Effective Communication in Remote Teams**: Clear and consistent communication is essential for remote teams. Choose the right communication tools, practice good video conferencing and instant

messaging etiquette, and actively work to build strong team connections. Address miscommunication proactively and handle conflicts with empathy and understanding.
4. **Maintaining Work-Life Balance**: Set clear boundaries between work and personal life to avoid burnout. Incorporate mindfulness practices to manage stress and maintain mental well-being. Work-life integration, rather than strict separation, can lead to a more fulfilling and balanced lifestyle.
5. **Long-term Success and Growth**: Remote work offers unique opportunities for career development. Continuously build your skills, network effectively, and seek out new opportunities to advance your career. Stay adaptable to change and keep an eye on future trends to ensure long-term success.

Final Tips for Thriving Remotely

As you continue your journey in remote work, keep these final tips in mind:

- **Stay Connected**: Isolation can be a challenge in remote work. Make a conscious effort to stay connected with your colleagues, friends, and professional network.
- **Be Proactive**: Take charge of your career by seeking out learning opportunities, asking for feedback, and volunteering for new challenges.
- **Prioritize Well-being**: Your mental and physical health should always be a priority. Make time for activities that help you relax and recharge, and don't hesitate to seek support when needed.
-

- **Embrace Flexibility**: One of the greatest advantages of remote work is flexibility. Use it to your advantage by creating a schedule that works for you and allows you to pursue both your professional and personal goals.

- **Keep Learning**: The world of work is constantly evolving, and continuous learning is key to staying competitive. Commit to lifelong learning and stay curious about new developments in your field.

Resources for Continued Learning

Your journey in mastering remote work doesn't end here. There are numerous resources available to help you continue learning and growing in this area:

- **Books**:
    - *"Remote: Office Not Required"* by Jason Fried and David Heinemeier Hansson
    - *"Deep Work: Rules for Focused Success in a Distracted World"* by Cal Newport
    - *"Atomic Habits: An Easy & Proven Way to Build Good Habits & Break Bad Ones"* by James Clear

- **Online Courses**:
    - *Productivity Masterclass* on Skillshare
    - *Time Management for Professionals* on LinkedIn Learning
    - *Mindfulness and Stress Management* on Coursera

- **Podcasts**:
    - *The Remote Work Podcast* by Andreas Klinger
    - *The Tim Ferriss Show* – particularly episodes on productivity and work-life balance
    - *WorkLife with Adam Grant* – focusing on the psychology of work
- **Blogs and Websites**:
    - *Zapier's Blog* on remote work tips and tools
    - *Trello Blog* for productivity and project management tips
    - *Buffer's Blog* on remote work culture and strategies

By continuing to explore these resources, you'll stay informed about best practices, new tools, and emerging trends in remote work, positioning yourself for ongoing success.

Remote work is more than just a temporary solution; it's a new way of thinking about work and life. By following the strategies outlined in this guide, you can build a fulfilling, successful career that allows you to achieve your goals while maintaining a healthy, balanced lifestyle. Embrace the flexibility and opportunities that remote work offers, and continue to learn and grow in this exciting new era of work.

Appendices

Appendix A: Recommended Tools and Resources

To help you implement the strategies discussed in this guide, here's a list of recommended tools and resources that can enhance your productivity, communication, and well-being in a remote work environment.

Productivity Tools

- **Trello**: A visual task management tool that uses boards, lists, and cards to help you organize tasks and projects. Great for both personal task management and team collaboration.
- **Asana**: A comprehensive project management tool that allows you to track tasks, set deadlines, and collaborate with team members. Ideal for managing complex projects.
- **Todoist**: A simple yet powerful to-do list app that helps you organize tasks, set priorities, and track progress. It's perfect for individual productivity.
- **Notion**: An all-in-one workspace that combines notes, tasks, databases, and collaboration tools. Highly customizable and great for managing both work and personal projects.
- **RescueTime**: A time-tracking app that helps you understand how you spend your time on your computer, identify distractions, and improve your productivity.
-

Pomodone: A time management tool that integrates with other task management apps and uses the Pomodoro Technique to help you stay focused and productive.

Communication Platforms

-
  Slack: A popular instant messaging platform designed for teams. It allows for real-time communication, file sharing, and integrates with many other productivity tools.
-
  Microsoft Teams: A collaboration platform that combines chat, video conferencing, and file storage. It's especially useful for organizations already using Microsoft Office products.
-
  Zoom: A leading video conferencing tool that's easy to use and reliable. It offers features like screen sharing, breakout rooms, and recording capabilities.
-
  Google Meet: A video conferencing tool that's integrated with Google Workspace, making it easy to schedule and join meetings from your calendar.
-
  Miro: A collaborative online whiteboard platform that's perfect for brainstorming sessions, team workshops, and visual collaboration.

Wellness and Mental Health Resources

-
  Headspace: A mindfulness and meditation app that offers guided sessions to help you reduce stress, increase focus, and improve sleep.
-

Calm: A mental wellness app that provides guided meditation, sleep stories, and relaxation techniques to help you manage stress and anxiety.

- **MyFitnessPal**: A health and fitness app that tracks your diet, exercise, and wellness goals, helping you maintain a healthy lifestyle while working remotely.

- **Stretchly**: A break reminder app that encourages you to take regular breaks, stretch, and move around during your workday to avoid burnout.

- **Talkspace**: An online therapy platform that connects you with licensed therapists via messaging, audio, and video sessions, offering mental health support when you need it.

Appendix B: Sample Templates and Checklists

To streamline your remote work routine and communication, here are some sample templates and checklists that you can customize to suit your needs.

Daily and Weekly Planning Templates

1. **Daily Planner Template**:
   - **Morning**: Review tasks and priorities, set goals for the day, and allocate time blocks for key tasks.
   - **Midday Check-In**: Assess progress, adjust priorities if needed, and take a break.
   - **Afternoon**: Focus on completing high-priority tasks, and wrap up the day with a brief review of what was accomplished.

End-of-Day: Plan for tomorrow, organize your workspace, and disconnect from work.

1. **Weekly Planner Template**:
   - **Monday**: Set weekly goals, prioritize tasks, and schedule meetings.
   - **Wednesday**: Mid-week review and adjustment of tasks and priorities.
   - **Friday**: Review weekly progress, reflect on achievements, and plan the next week.

Communication Protocols for Remote Teams

1. **Weekly Team Meeting Agenda Template**:
   - **Introduction**: Welcome and brief overview of the meeting agenda.
   - **Updates**: Team members share progress on tasks, highlight any blockers, and discuss solutions.
   - **Discussion**: Address key issues, brainstorm ideas, and collaborate on upcoming projects.
   - **Action Items**: Review and assign tasks for the following week.
   - **Closing**: Recap decisions made, summarize key takeaways, and schedule the next meeting.
1. **Instant Messaging Etiquette Checklist**:
   - **Use Clear Subject Lines**: Start conversations with a clear subject to help others understand the context quickly.

Be Concise: Keep messages short and to the point, avoiding unnecessary details.
  o
Respect Availability: Check the recipient's status before sending non-urgent messages.
  o
Use Channels Appropriately: Post messages in the appropriate channels to keep communication organized.
  o

Follow Up: If you don't receive a response in a reasonable time, follow up politely.

Work-Life Balance Checklist

1. **Setting Boundaries**:
   o
   Define clear start and end times for your workday.
   o
   Designate a specific workspace and avoid working in personal spaces.
   o
   Communicate your work hours to family members and colleagues.
1. **Managing Stress**:
   o
   Schedule regular breaks throughout your workday.
   o
   Incorporate mindfulness practices, such as meditation or deep breathing exercises.
   o
   Engage in physical activity or hobbies outside of work to relax and recharge.
1. **Integrating Work and Personal Life**:
   o
   Set goals that align both your professional and personal aspirations.

- Create a flexible schedule that accommodates personal commitments.
- Make time for hobbies and activities that bring you joy and fulfillment.

Appendix C: Further Reading and References

To deepen your understanding of remote work and continue learning, here are some recommended books, articles, blogs, podcasts, and videos.

Books, Articles, and Research Papers

- **Books**:
    - *"Remote: Office Not Required"* by Jason Fried and David Heinemeier Hansson
    - *"Deep Work: Rules for Focused Success in a Distracted World"* by Cal Newport
    - *"The 4-Hour Workweek"* by Tim Ferriss
    - *"Atomic Habits: An Easy & Proven Way to Build Good Habits & Break Bad Ones"* by James Clear
    - *"The Happiness Project"* by Gretchen Rubin
- **Articles and Research Papers**:
    - *"The Benefits and Challenges of Remote Work"* - Harvard Business Review

"How Remote Work Is Changing the Way We Work" - McKinsey & Company
o

"The Future of Remote Work: Trends and Predictions" - Deloitte Insights

Relevant Blogs and Websites

- **Zapier Blog**: Offers practical tips and tools for remote work productivity and automation.
- **Buffer Blog**: Focuses on remote work culture, strategies, and case studies from their fully remote team.
- **Trello Blog**: Provides insights on project management, team collaboration, and productivity in remote work.
- **Workplaceless**: A blog dedicated to remote work best practices, training, and career development.
- **Remote.co**: Features expert advice, Q&As, and resources for both remote workers and companies.

Podcasts and Videos on Remote Work

- **Podcasts**:
    - *The Remote Work Podcast* by Andreas Klinger: Discussions on remote work trends, tools, and best practices.
    - *WorkLife with Adam Grant*: Explores the psychology of work and offers insights on productivity and workplace culture.

- *The Tim Ferriss Show*: Interviews with top performers, including tips on productivity, work-life balance, and personal development.
- *The Productivity Show* by Asian Efficiency: Focuses on time management, productivity techniques, and tools for remote workers.

- **Videos**:
  - "How to Work Remotely and Still Get Things Done" - TEDx Talk by Liam Martin
  - "The Future of Work Is Remote" - TEDx Talk by John Spencer
  - "Tips for Working from Home" - YouTube series by Google Workspace
  - "Mindfulness and Productivity" - YouTube series by Calm

By utilizing the tools, templates, and resources provided in these appendices, you can further enhance your remote work experience and continue to grow both personally and professionally. Whether you're seeking to boost your productivity, improve communication with your team, or maintain a healthy work-life balance, these resources will support your journey towards long-term success in the digital workspace.

www.ingramcontent.com/pod-product-compliance
Lightning Source LLC
Chambersburg PA
CBHW070419230526
45471CB00006B/2883